DOUBLE-CRESTED CORMORANTS

Studies for Wildlife Artists

Photography and Text

by

Al Lodwick

DEDICATION

To Ann Lodwick, my wife and best friend for nearly thirty-eight years.

ACKNOWLEDGEMENTS

Scott Mies for encouragement and editorial advice.

Rachel Lodwick for the Mieswick, LLC logo.

Victoria Tubbs for the author's photograph.

INTRODUCTION

This book is the result of five years of nature photography in the biologically diverse central highlands of Arizona around Prescott. The Arizona highlands are not what most people imagine when they first think of Arizona. At the lowest level you find desert grassland. This gives way to Oak-Pinyon-Juniper woodland. Higher still are the tall Ponderosa Pines – a stand of trees stretching hundreds of miles in Arizona and New Mexico. At the highest levels you find Douglas Fir forest. Throughout the highlands you find an intermingling of both flora and fauna from both hotter and colder climates. For example, you can find hedgehog cacti growing at the roots of Ponderosa Pines.

Perched in dead Ponderosa Pines and swimming in reservoirs you will find the Double-crested Cormorant. Though not abundant, they are commonly seen by even those taking causal walks or jogging along the shores.

The emphasis of this book is to depict scenes for wildlife artists that are not easily seen with the unaided eye. Examples of this are the actions of the feet when taking off from water, the actions of the wings and tail when taking off from trees, how the wings look in flight and perhaps, the most challenging of all, the extensive black coloring that needs to be just right.

The author hopes that non-artists will also enjoy the pictures and learn more about these magnificent birds and the habitats of the highlands of central Arizona.

Al Lodwick
Prescott, Arizona
June 2015

PERCHING

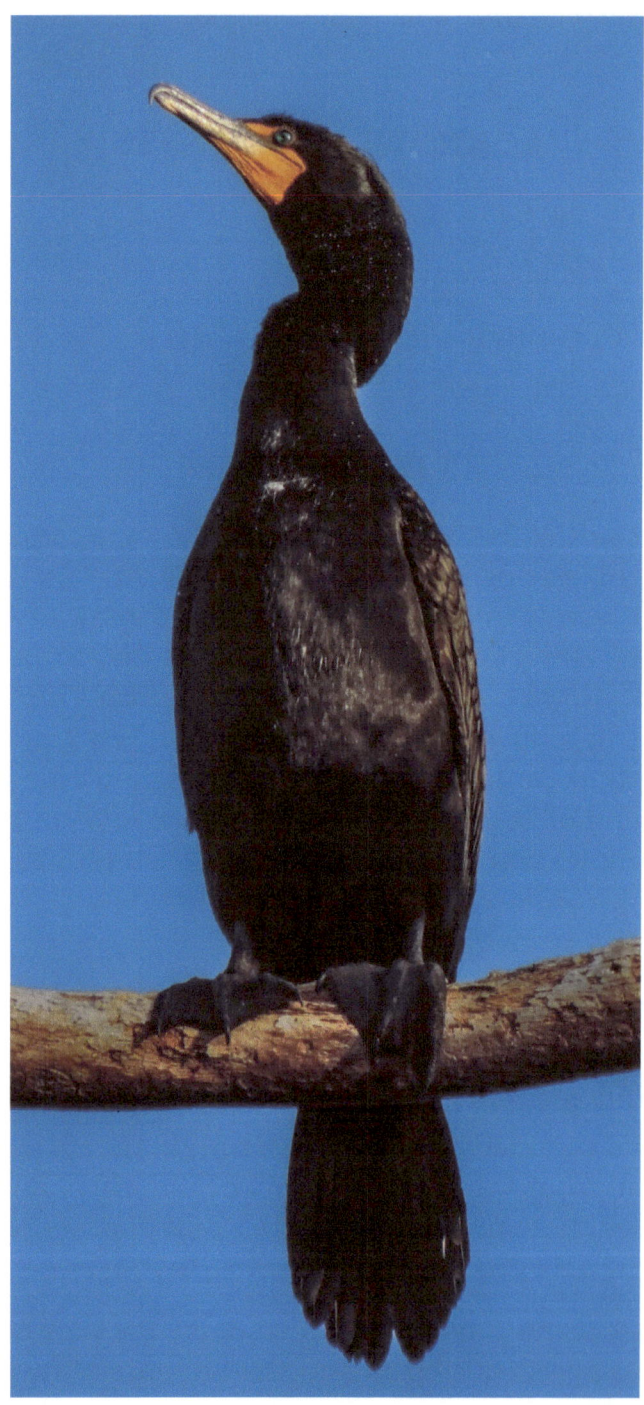

       Double-crested Cormorants lack oil glands that keep their feathers from becoming waterlogged. Over time they sink lower and lower in the water as they pursue fish. Consequently, they are often seen perched in trees, preening and drying out in preparation for their next foray.

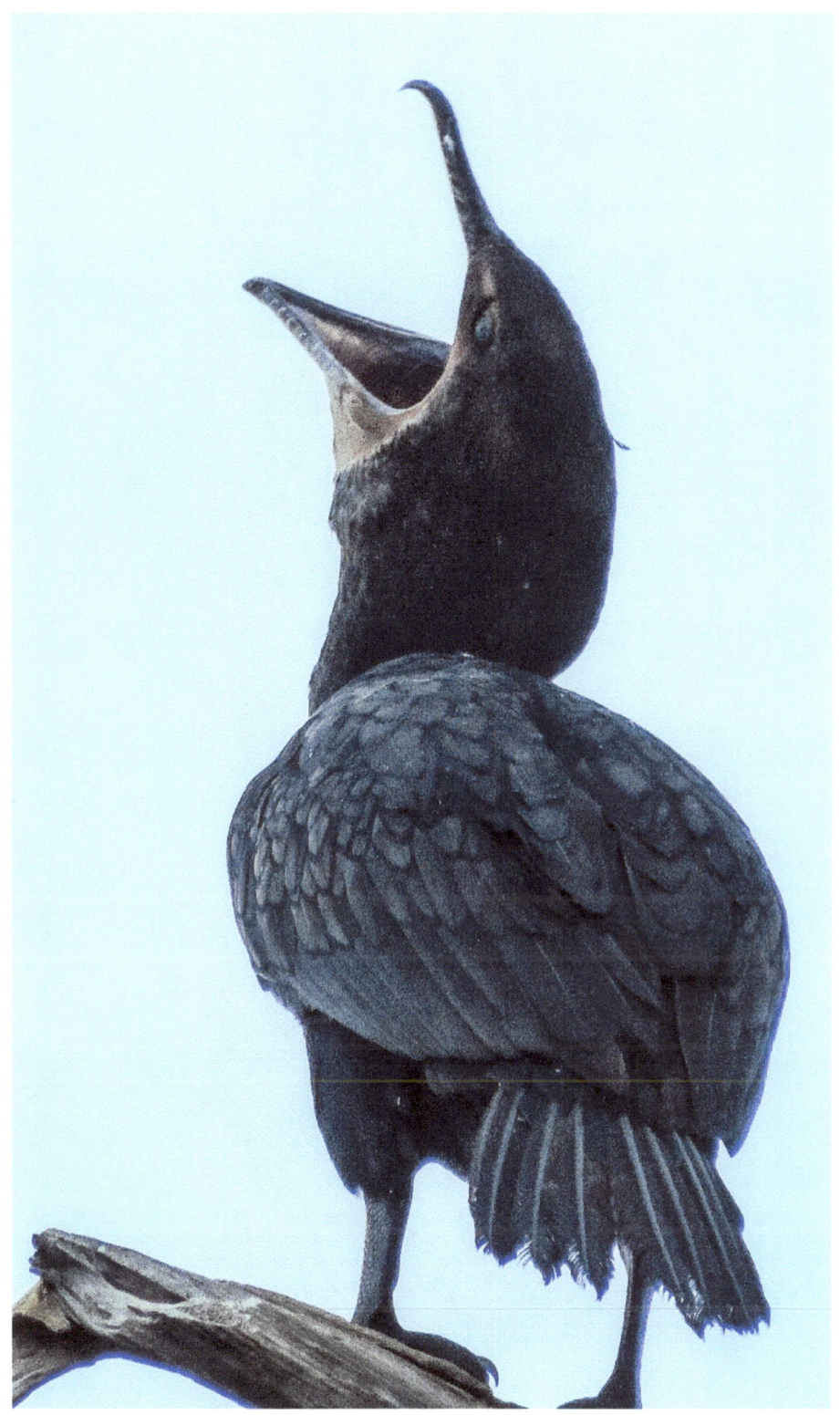

As you can see, Double-crested Cormorants have huge mouths. Note too, the prominent hook on the end of their bill for catching and holding their prey. Displaying the blue lining of the inside of the mouth is one way that male Double-crested Cormorants attract females.

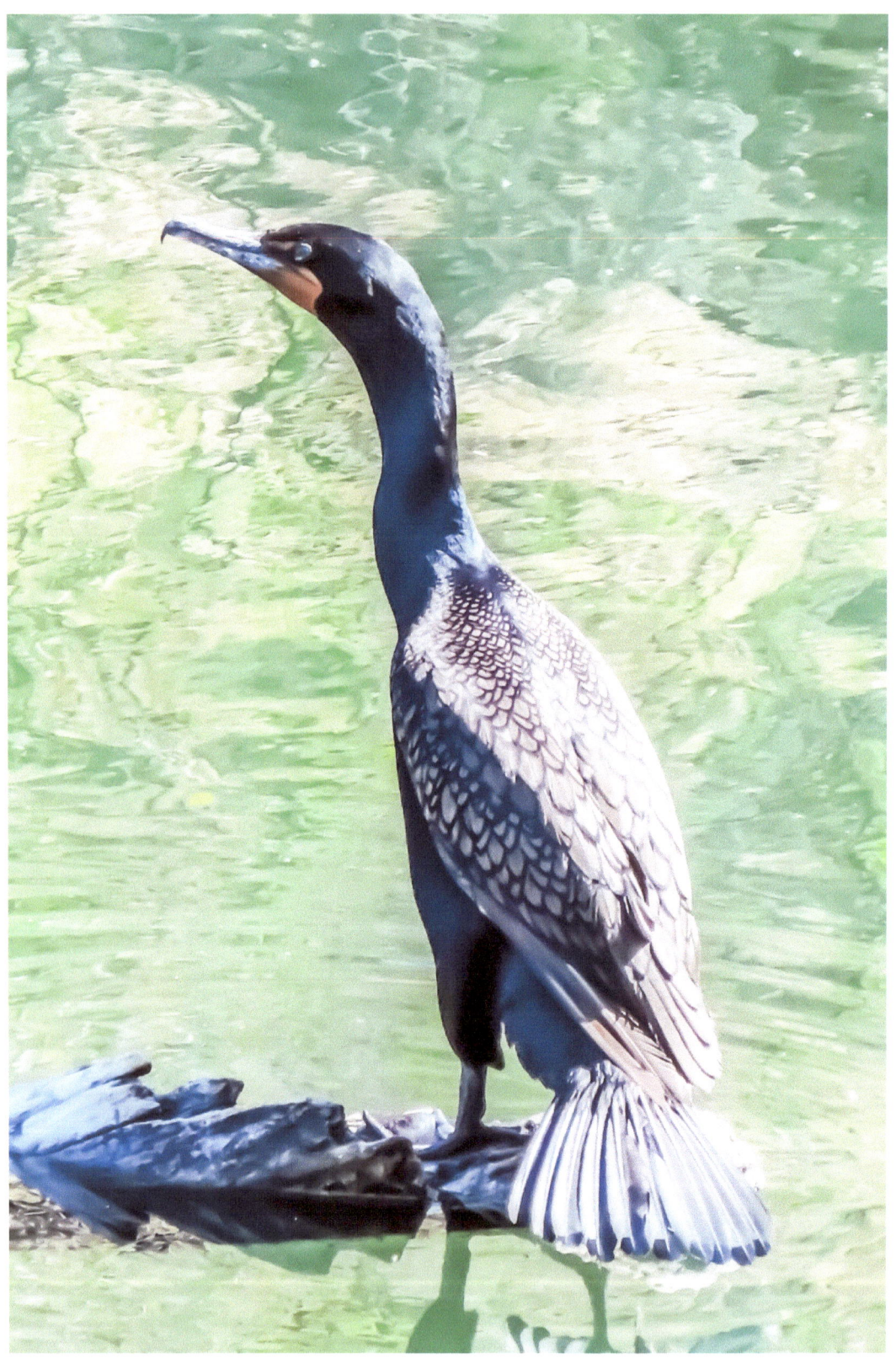

A typical posture of a Double-crested Cormorant sitting on a rock in the water drying its feathers.

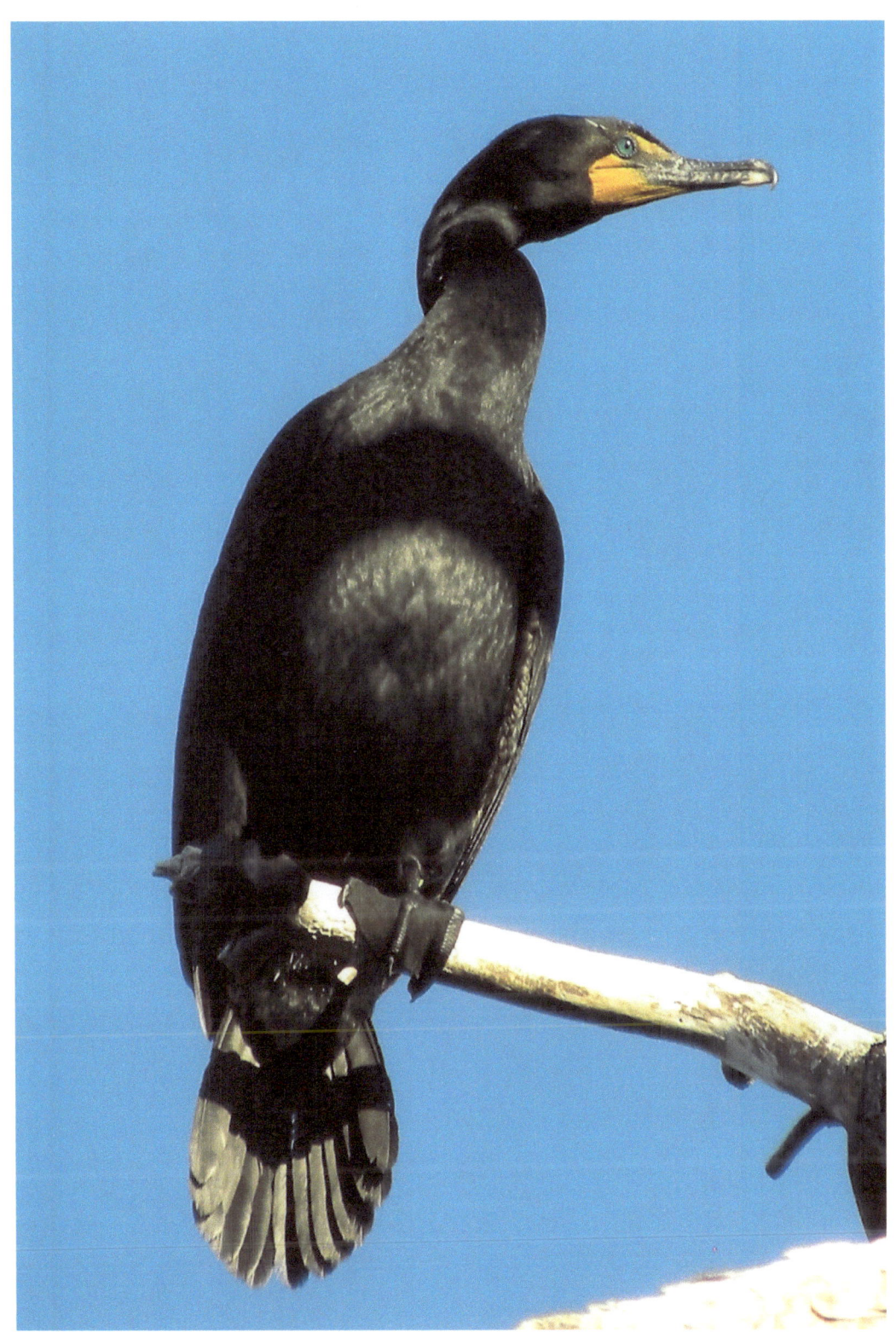

This picture illustrates how the webbed feet of the Double-crested Cormorant grasp the limb of a dead tree. The webbed feet are used to pursue fish underwater. The birds can stay underwater for about a minute without coming up for air.

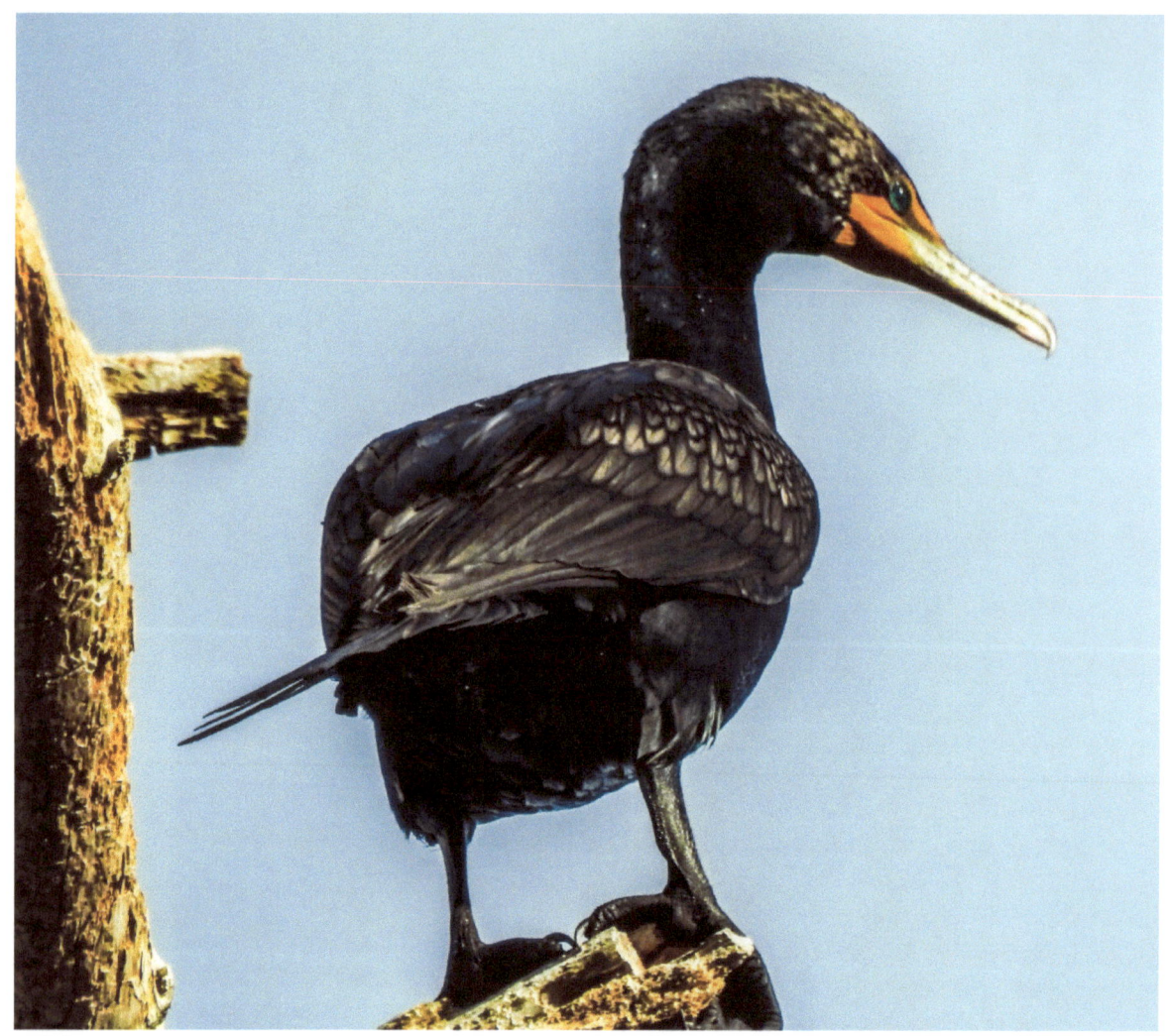

The back of this Double-crested Cormorant shows a good example of how the wing feathers are composed and how they are layered.

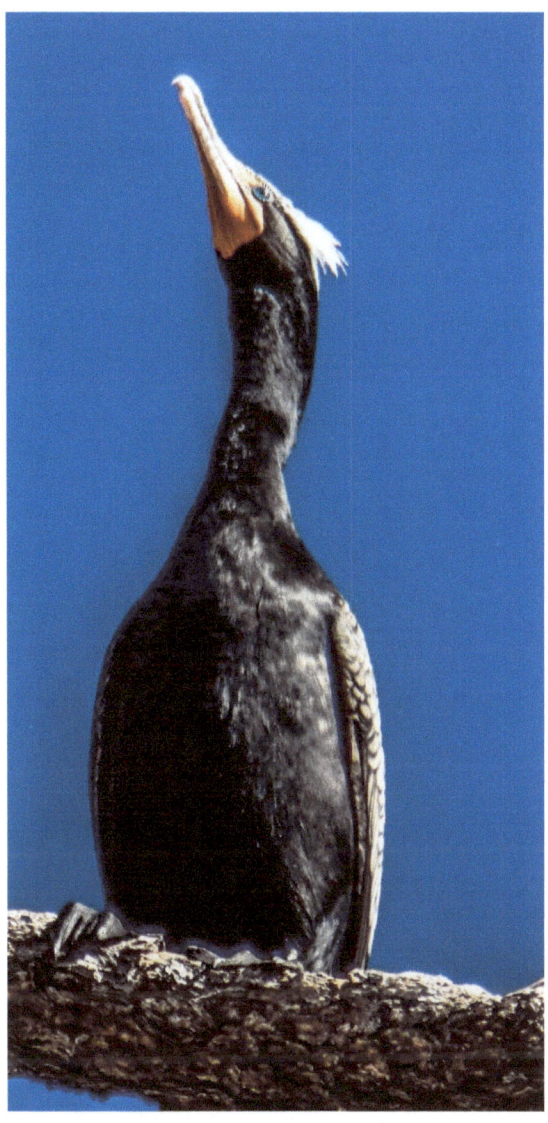

The crests from which the common name for these birds is derived may be white, black or a mixture depending on their genetic makeup.

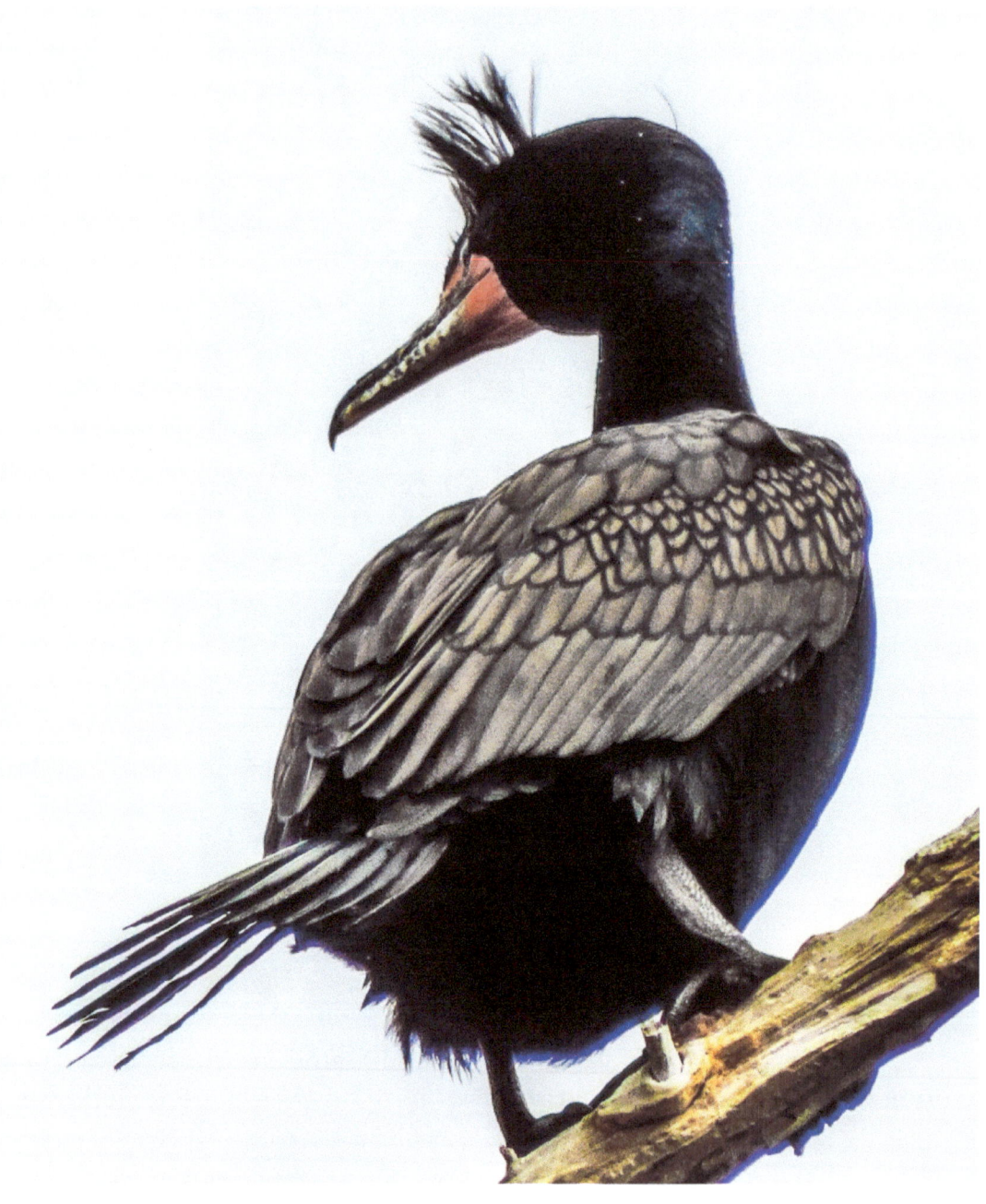

Look closely at this Double-crested Cormorant's right leg and you will see the pattern of the scales on it.

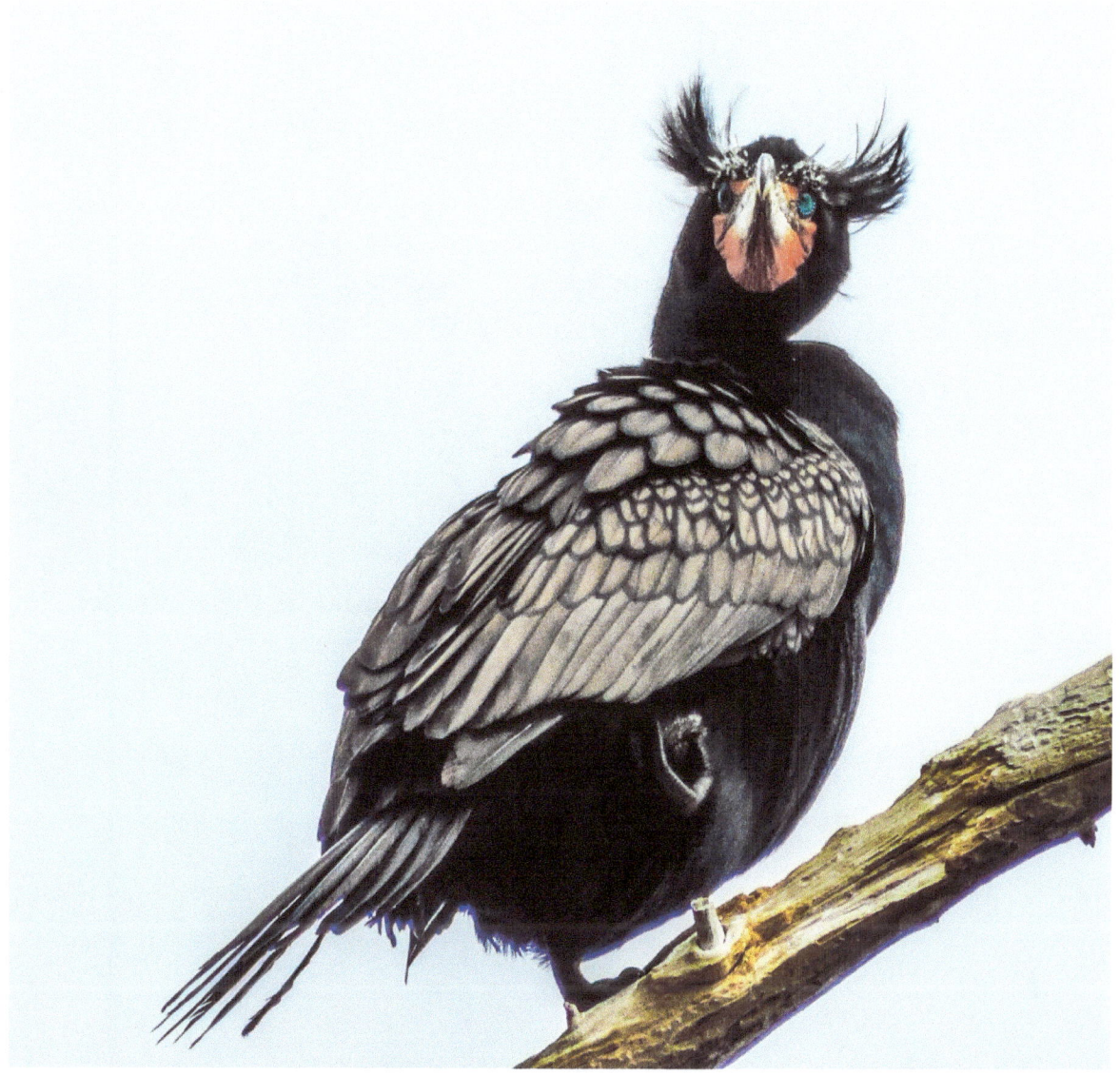

In addition to the black and white feathers in this bird's crest also note the odd look of its right foot as it balances on its left foot and the worn condition of its tail feathers.

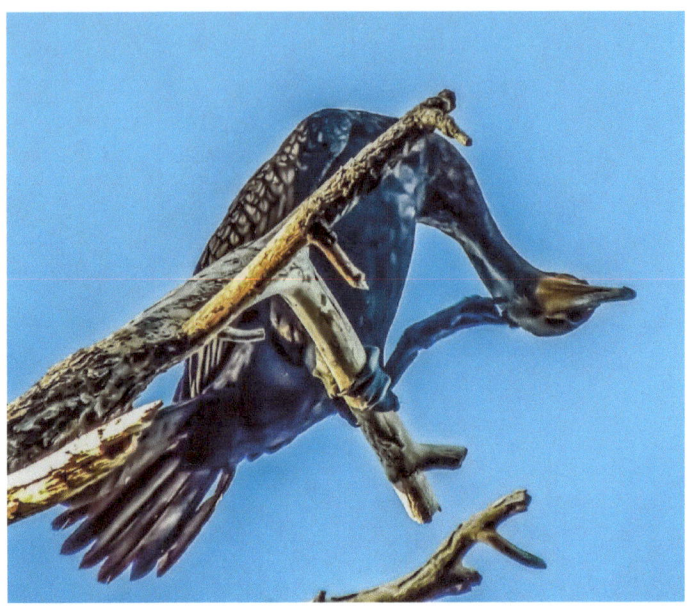

When it itches you have just got to scratch could be the motto for this Double-crested Cormorant.

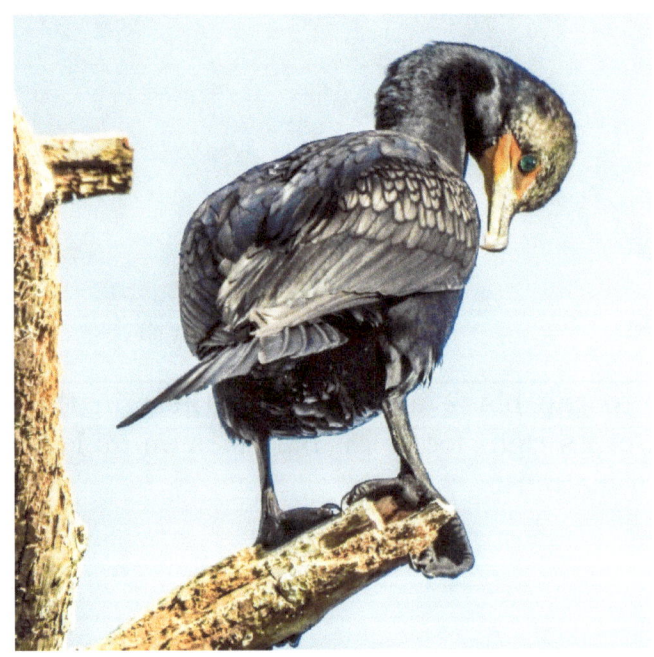

These birds spend a lot of time preening.

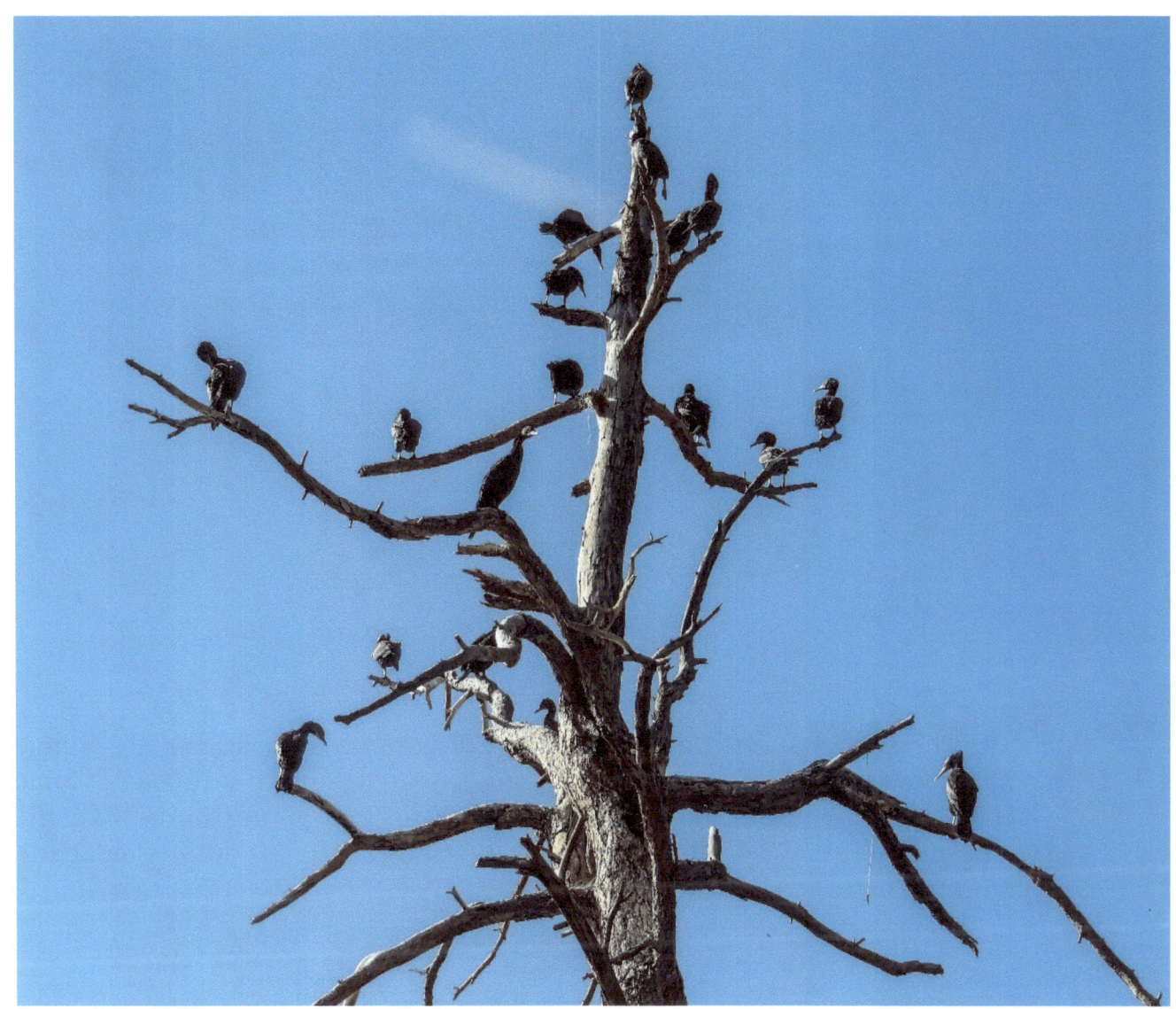

When fish are abundant, Double-crested Cormorants will congregate in great numbers. This tree on the shore of Lynx Lake in Arizona is commonly referred to as, "the cormorant tree". It is possible that this tree was killed by the droppings of the birds just as over-fertilizing a lawn will kill it.

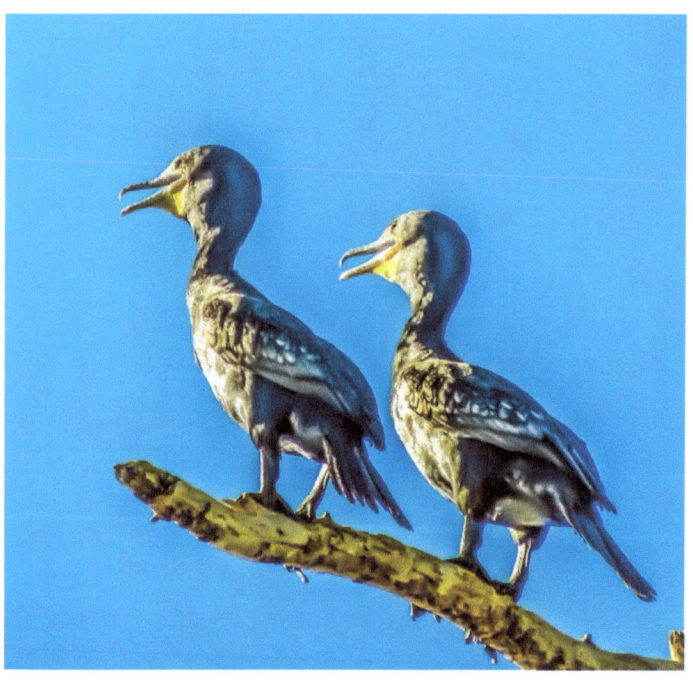

These immature Double-crested Cormorants almost exactly mimic each other as they appear to be awaiting the arrival of an adult with some food. Adults deposit food into the mouths of very young birds. As the young mature, they switch to inserting their head into the adult's mouth to obtain the regurgitated fish.

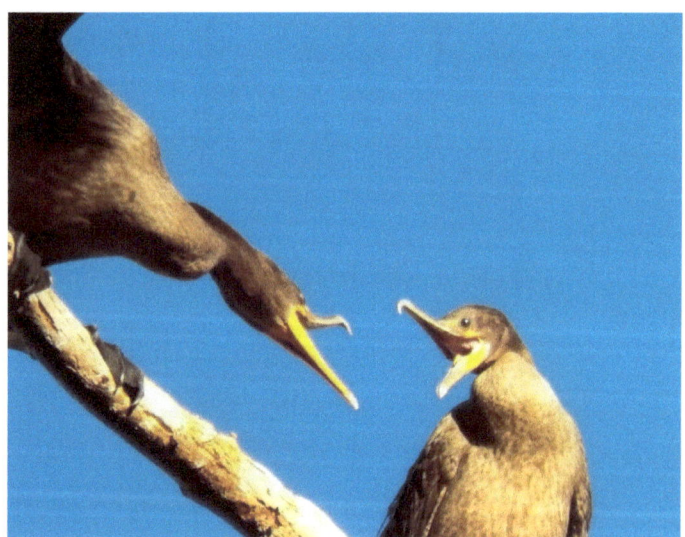

Before the adult arrives with food, a dispute erupts – probably over who is higher in the pecking order.

SWIMMING

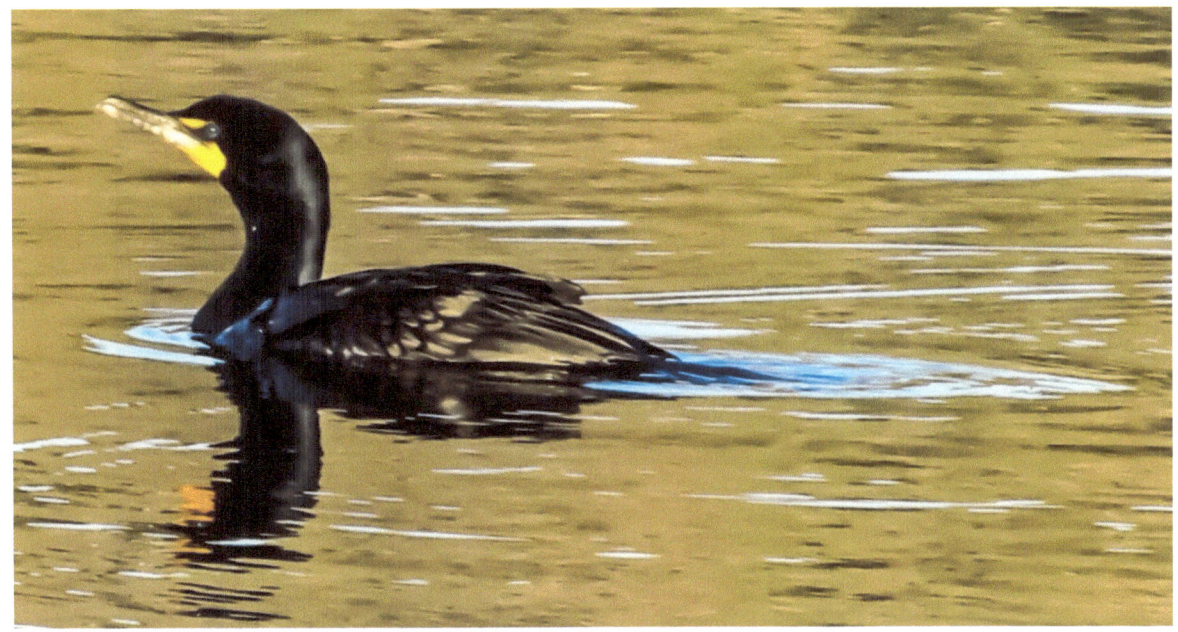

    Since Double-crested Cormorants lack oil to keep their feathers dry they tend to swim lower in the water than most other waterfowl. The longer they stay in the water the more they sink.

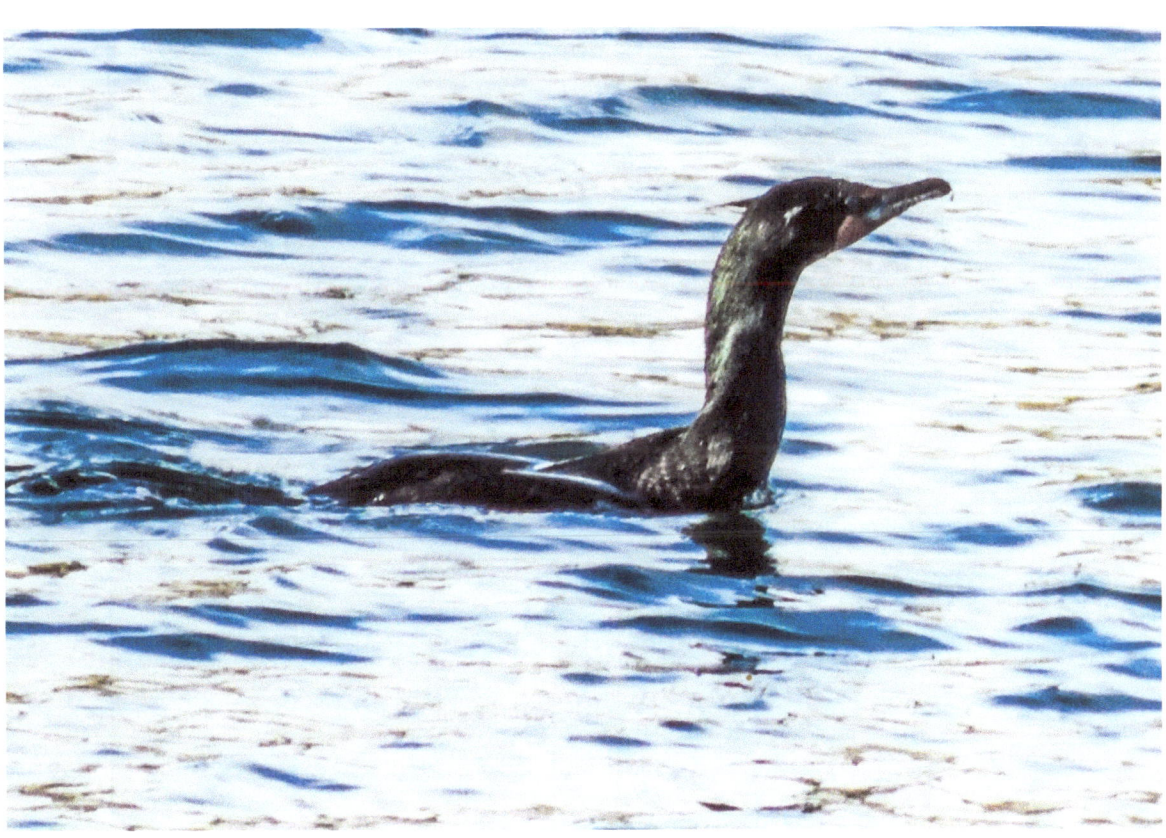

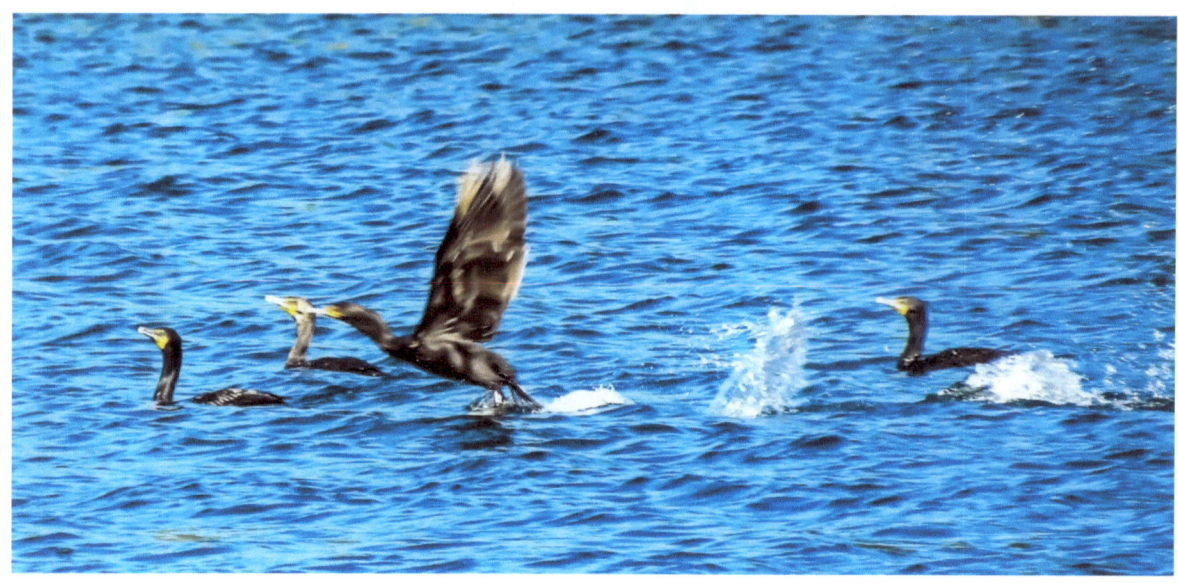

When they pursue fish, Double-crested Cormorants simply put their head underwater and submerge. They use their webbed feet to propel themselves after the fish. Most fish are swallowed underwater. After several dives they are quite waterlogged. In order to take-off in this condition they need to run about ten steps across the surface of the water to gain speed. You could picture a series of these splashes with each one smaller than the next one closer to the bird.

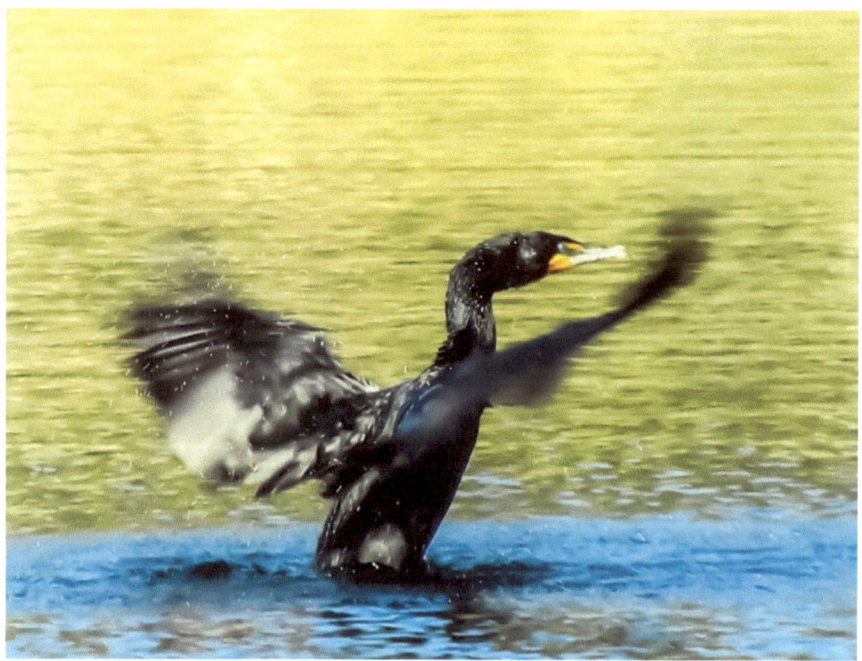

Occasionally a bird will just rise up and shake off some of the accumulated water from its feathers.

FLYING

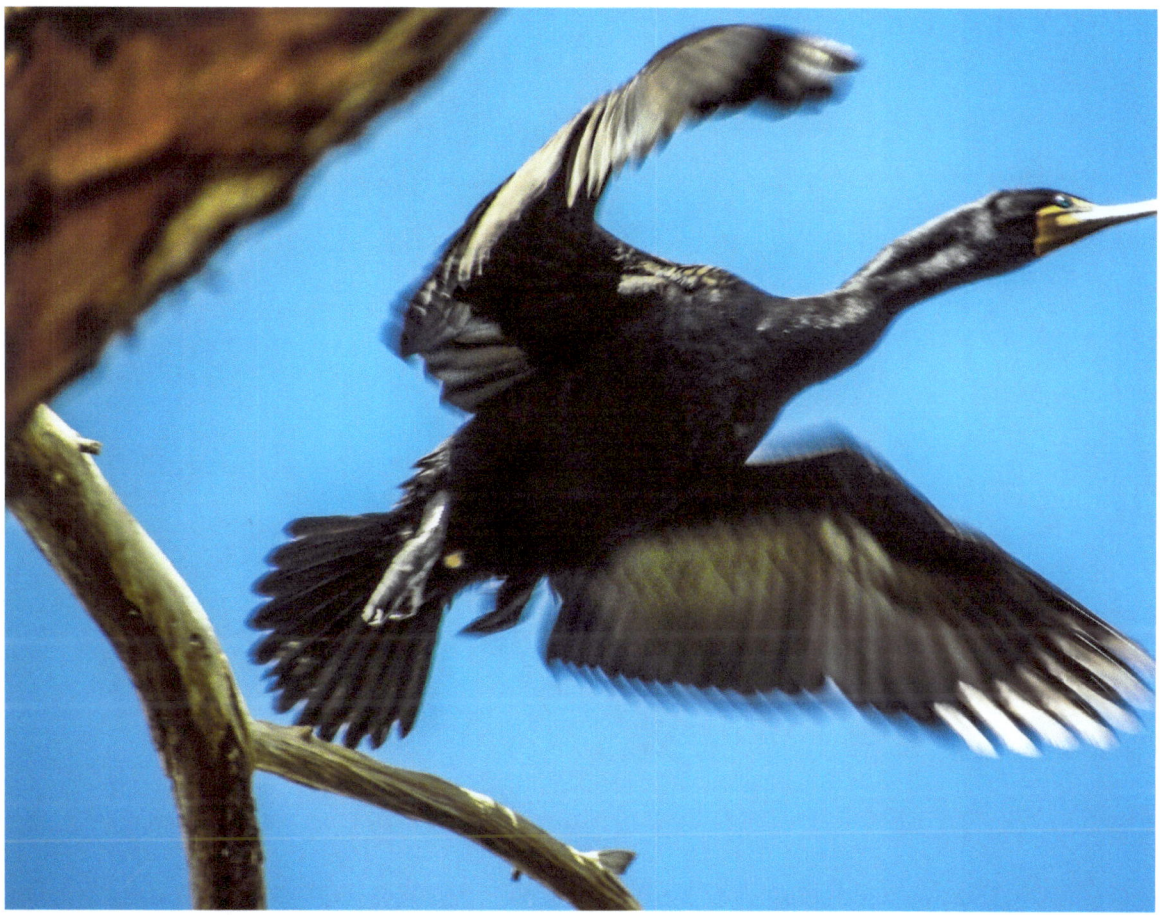

    Here we see the majority of the bird as it takes its first wing beat after jumping off the branch of a dead Ponderosa Pine. The wing tips should not be pictured as white, they are reflecting light that makes them appear lighter than they are.

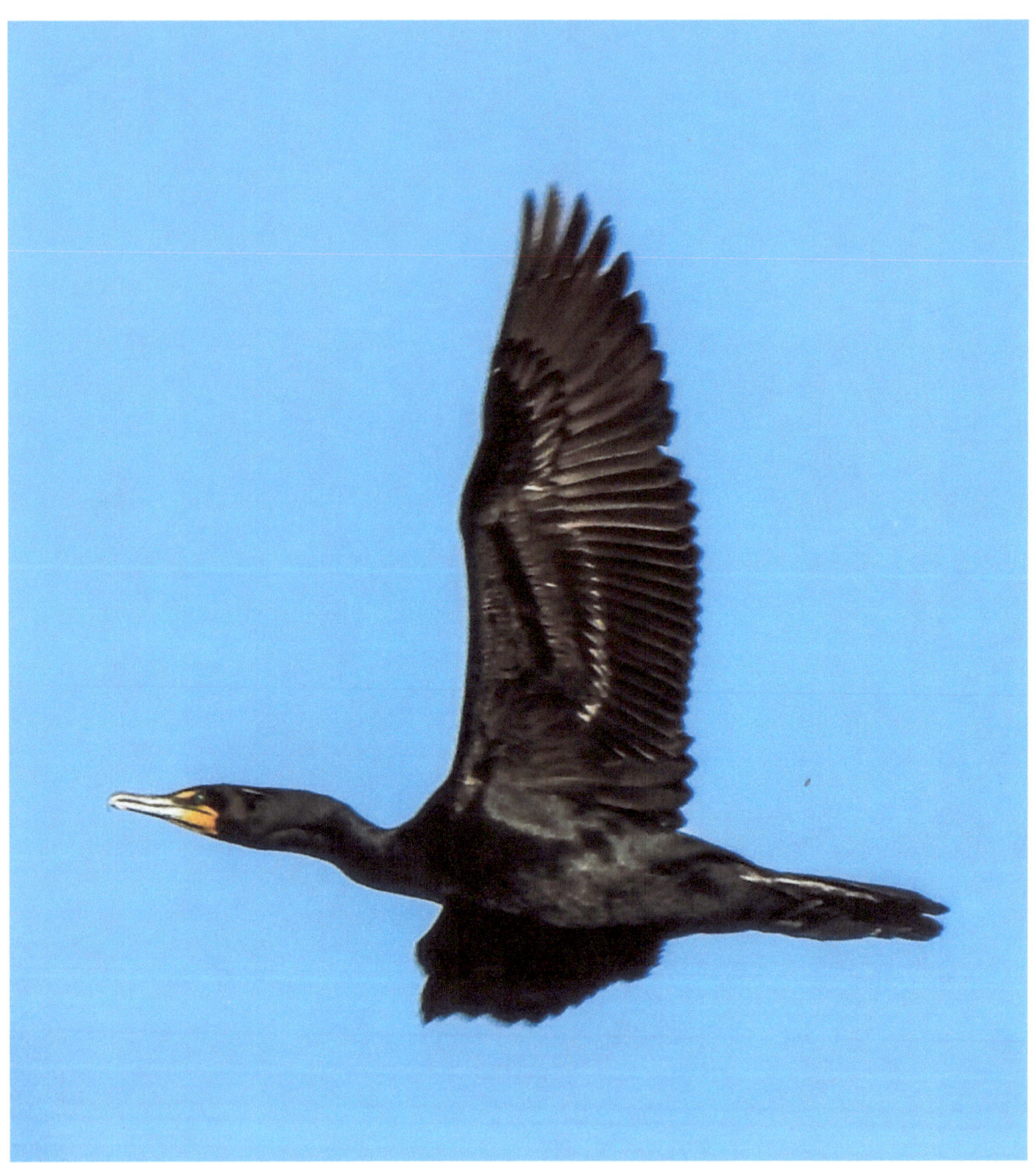

In-flight the two main things that you notice about Double-crested Cormorants is how far back on their body that their wings are set and how rapidly they must flap their wings to stay aloft.

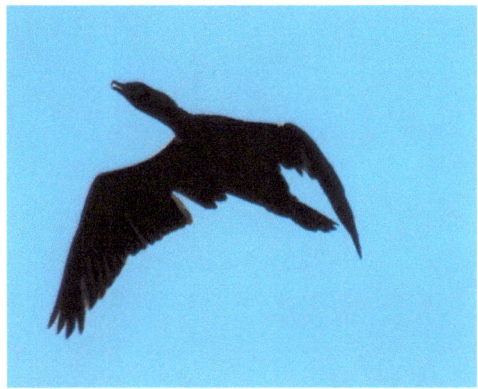

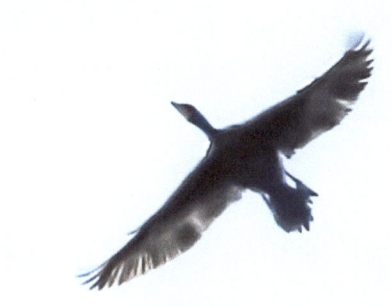

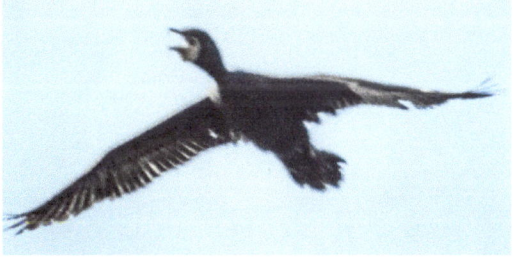

These silhouettes are included for the artist to be able to get the wings and in particular the primary feathers "just right" and the unusual activity of flying with an open mouth.

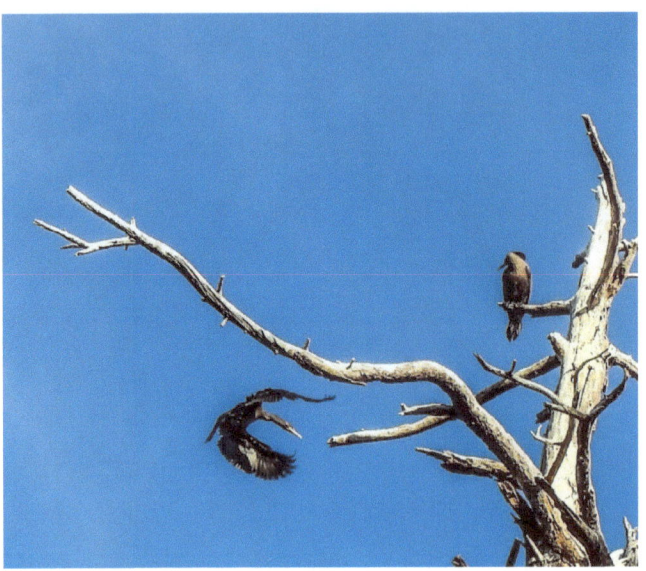

This picture illustrates the position of the wings and head as a Double-crested Cormorant is landing in a dead Ponderosa Pine.

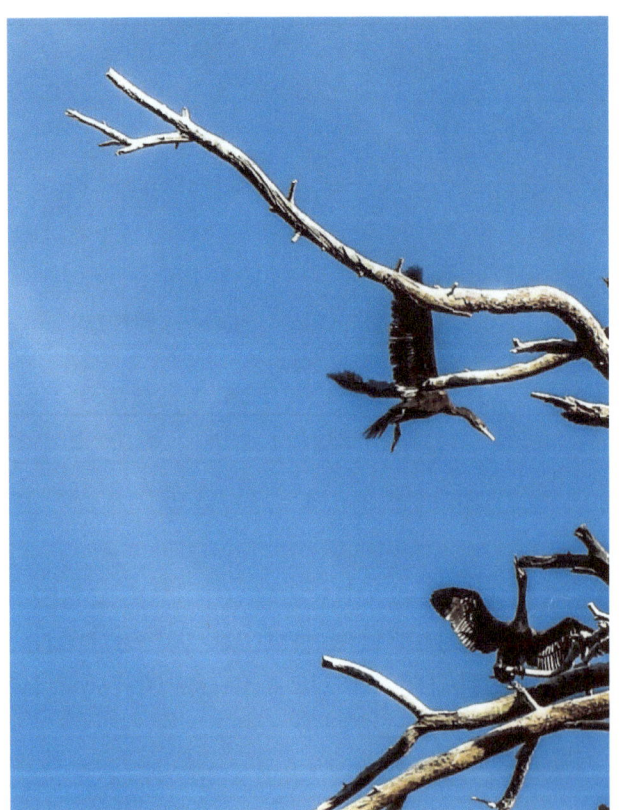

This is the same bird as in the upper picture less than a second later. Note the position of the head, wings and feet as it gets closer to landing. Also note that the bird below it is alert to be sure there in no encroaching on its territory.

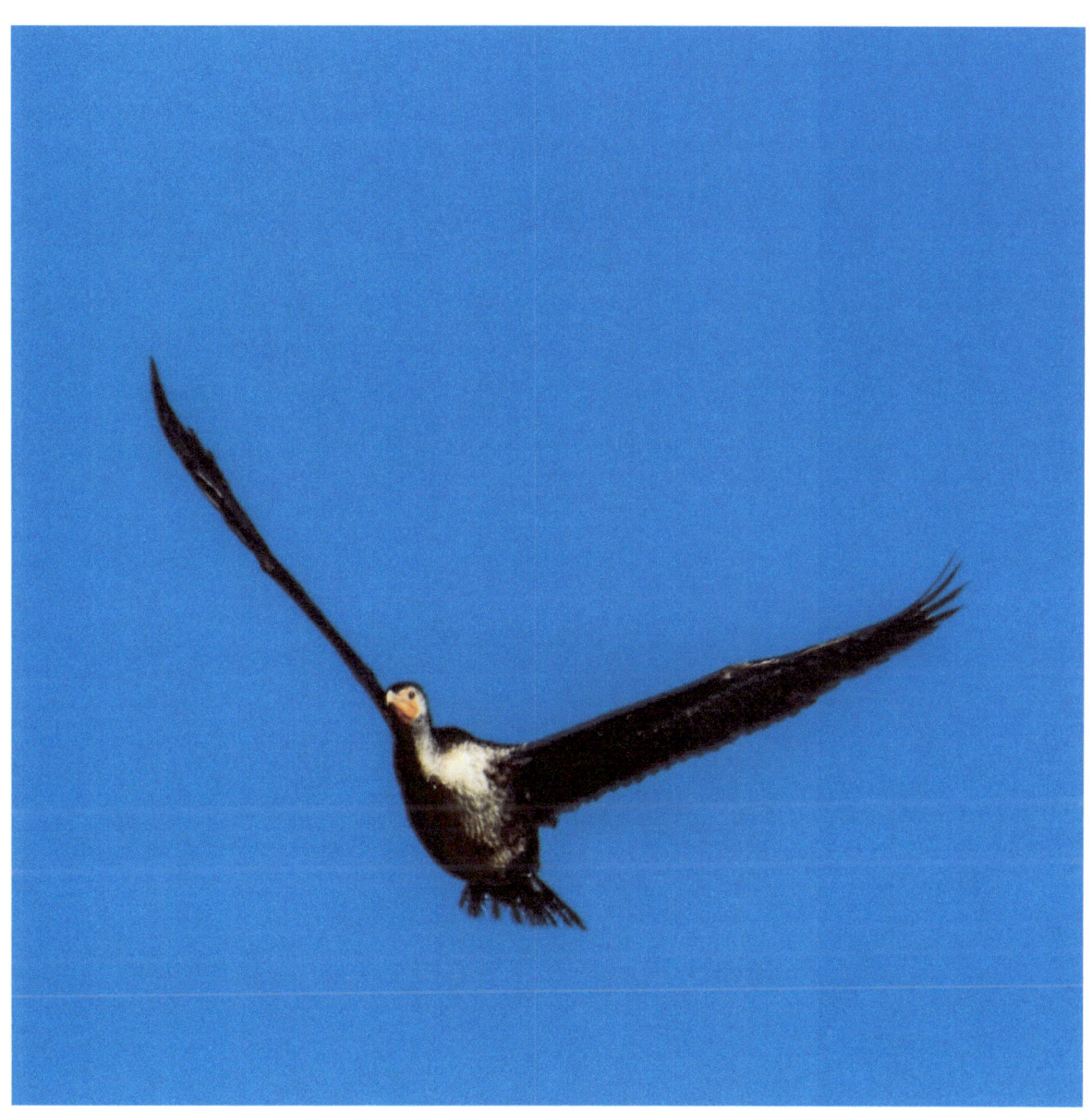

Double-crested Cormorants are a little under 3 feet in length and have a wingspan of over 4 feet. They weigh about 4 to 5 pounds, Males and females look alike.

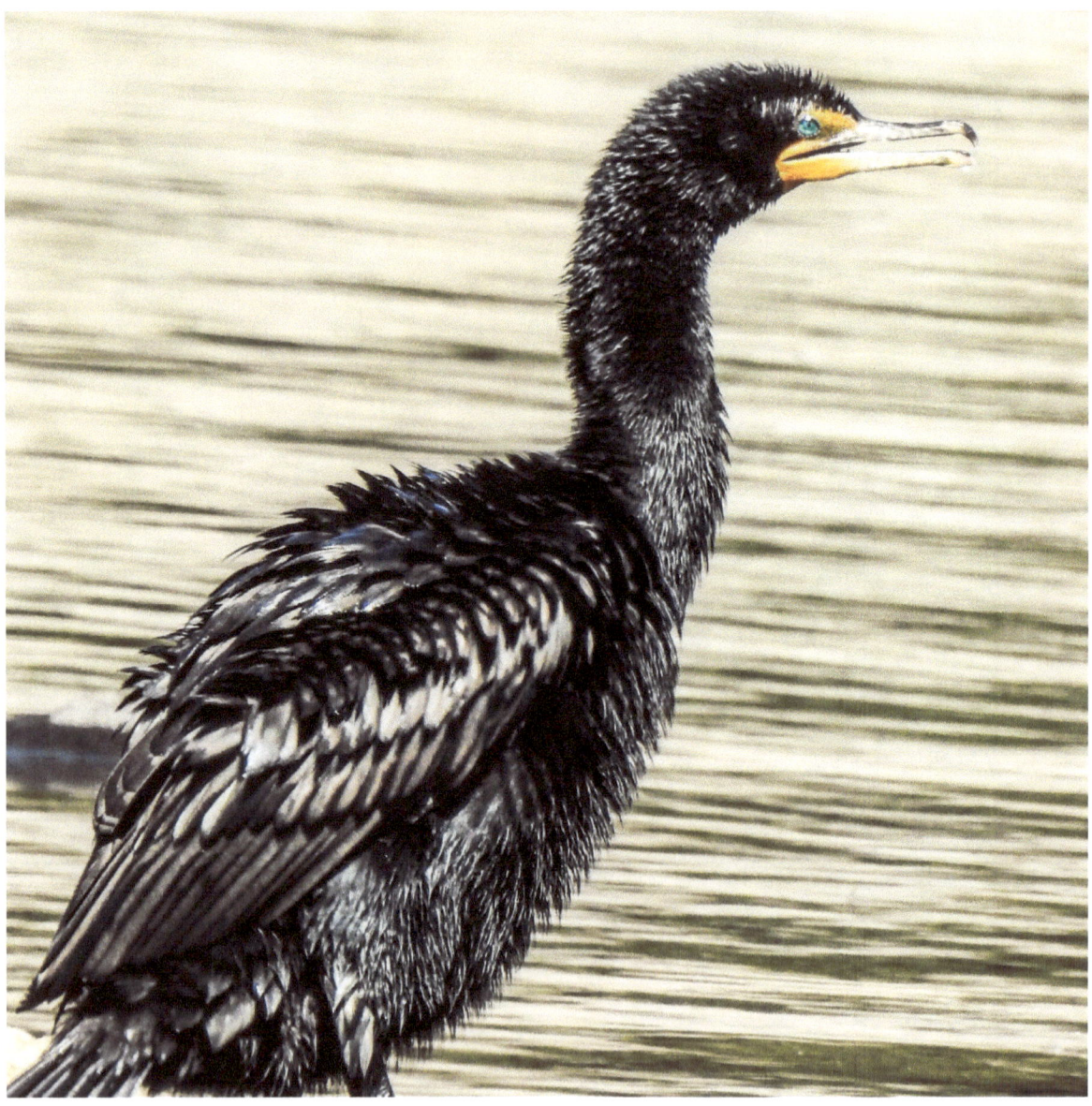

This bird has just emerged from the water. Its feathers are completely waterlogged.

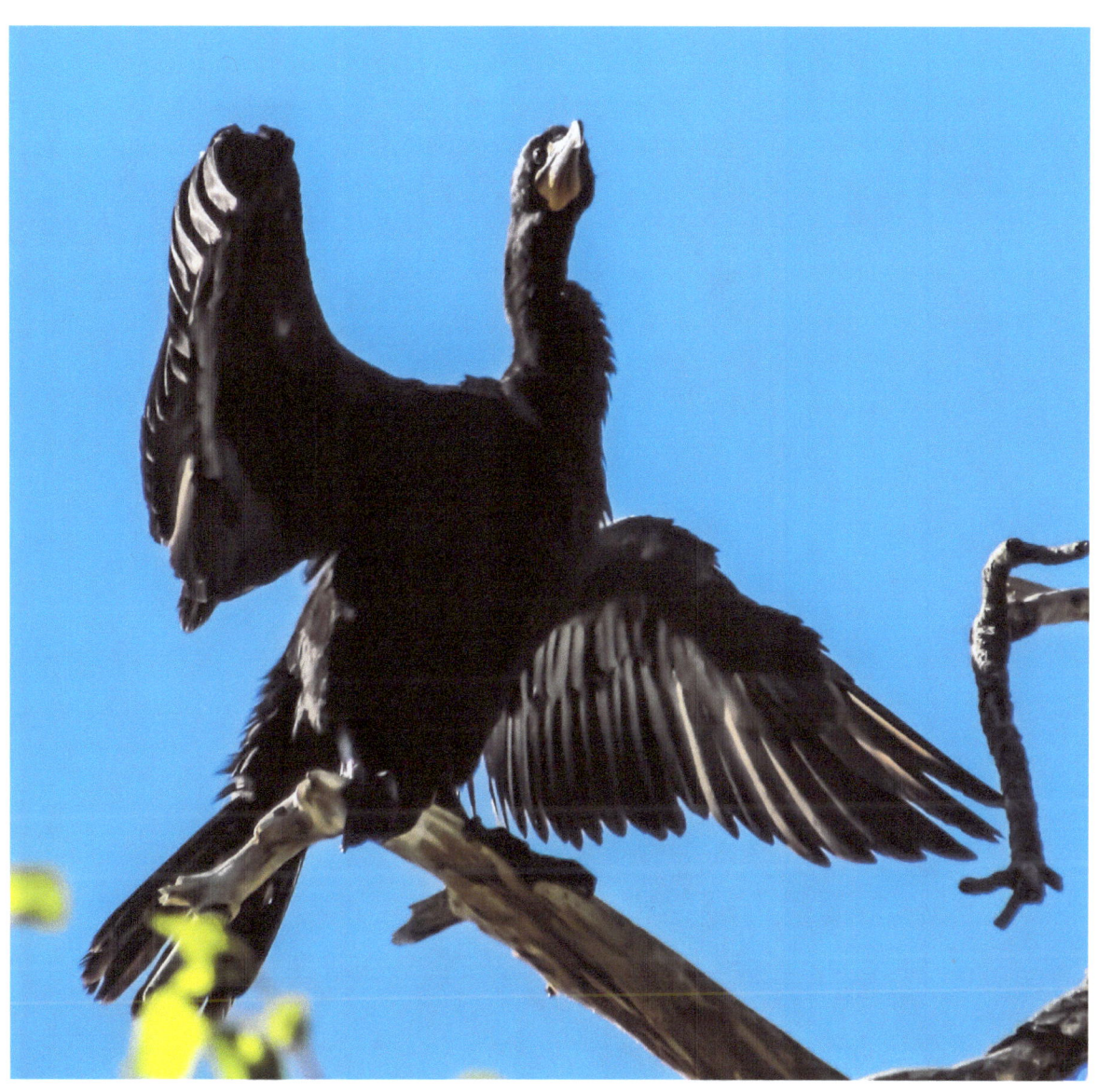

It appears as though this Double-crested Cormorant is about to take flight but it is actually drying its wings. Having its back to the morning sun speeds the drying process.

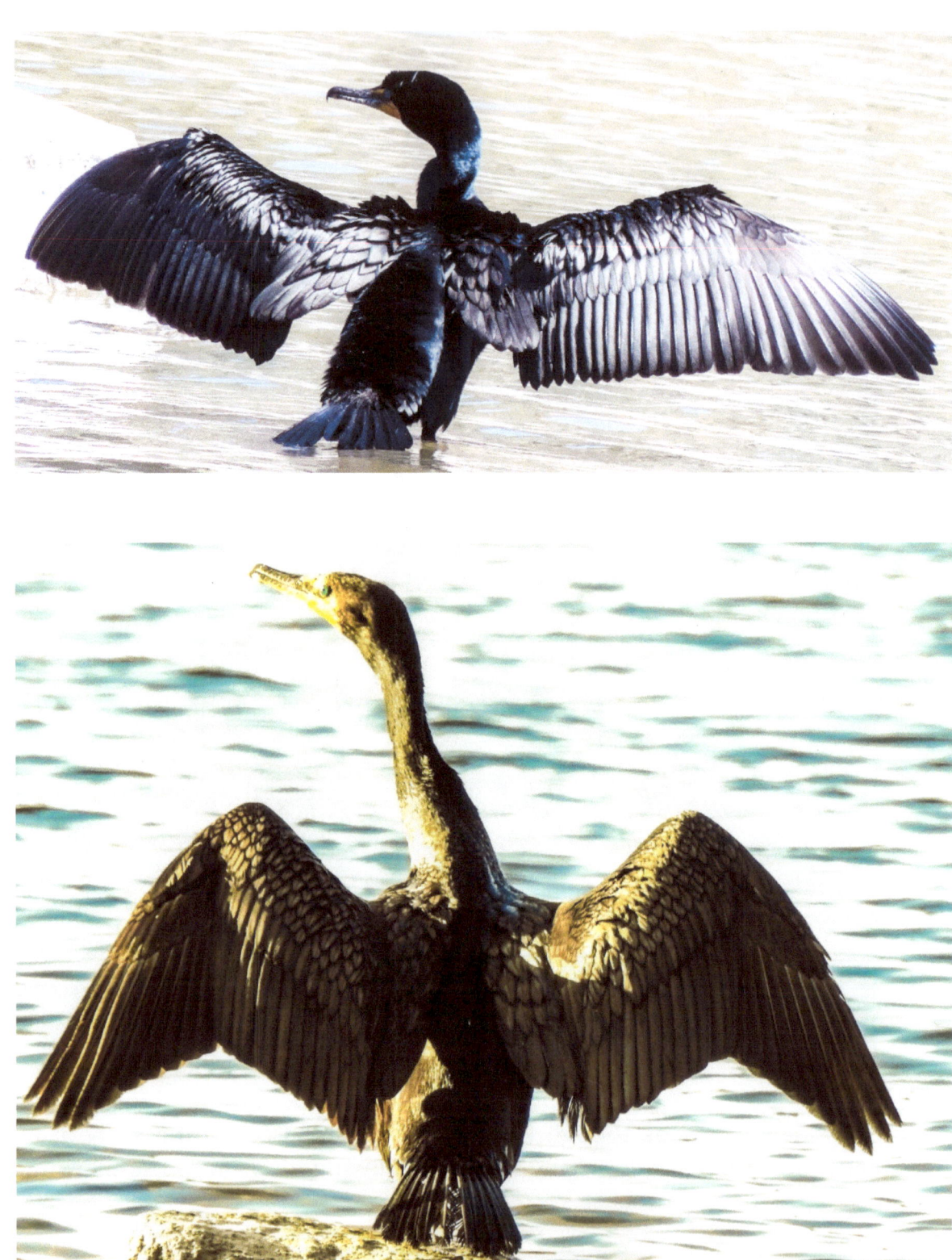

More wing drying activity. The brownish color of the lower bird indicates that it a juvenile in its first summer of life.

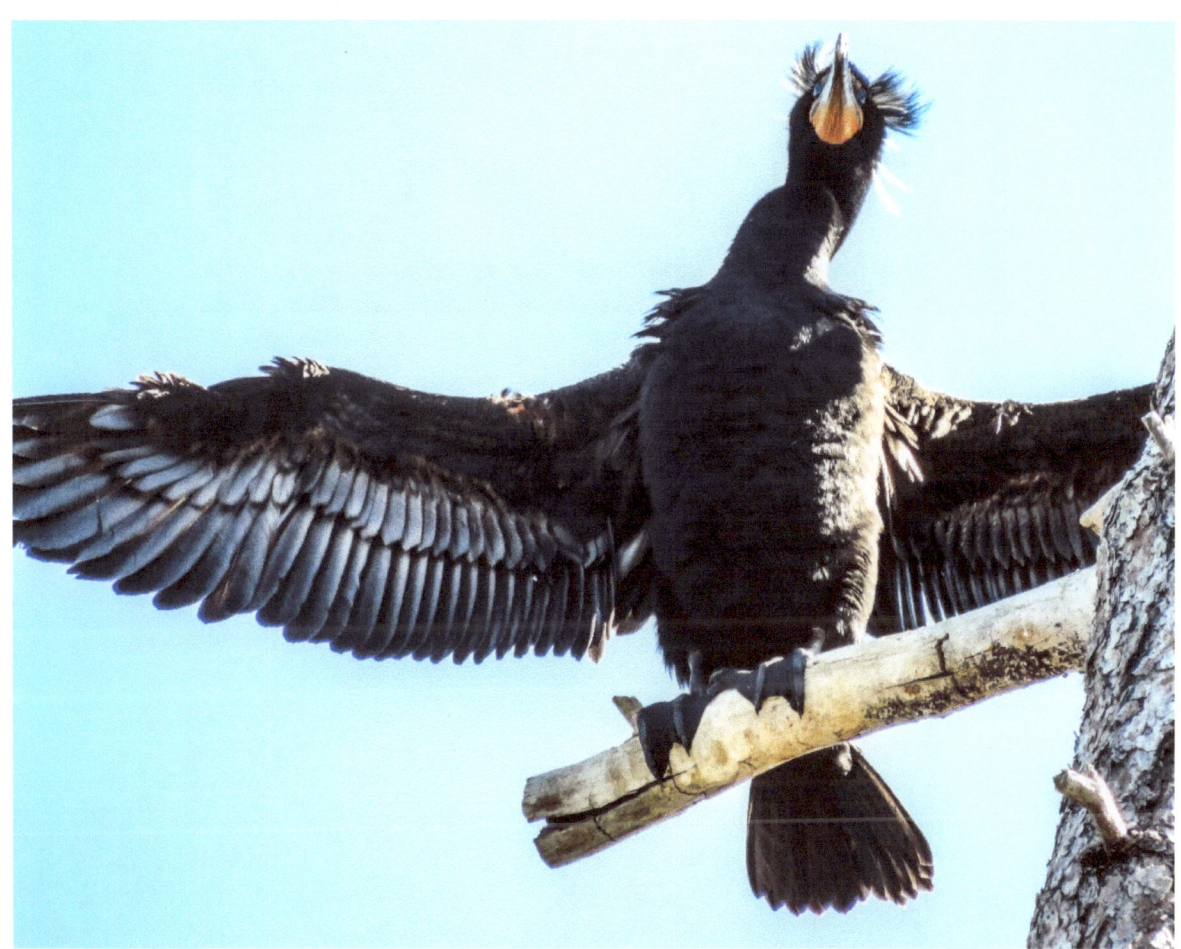

     This picture shows many elements of a perched, drying Double-crested Cormorant in breeding plumage. The crests can be either black or white and this bird has both. The feathers on the underside of the wing are shown as are the feathers over the wing joints. Finally the webbed feet and the spread of the tail are illustrated.

HEADS

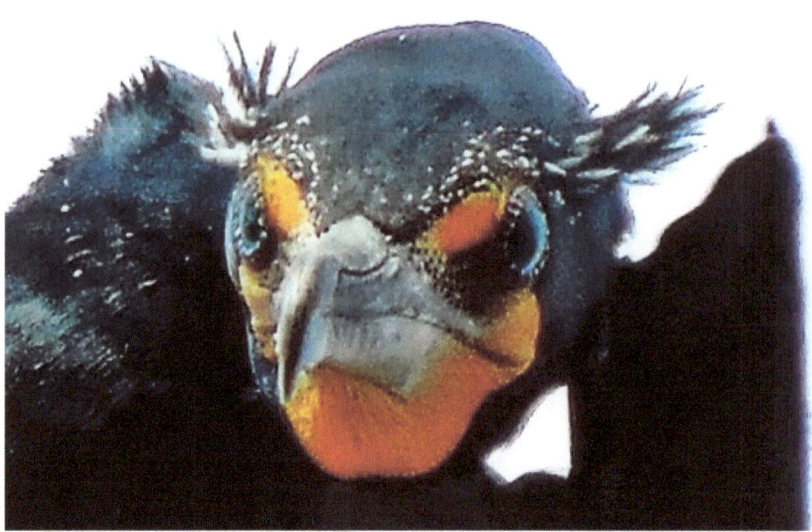

It would seem reasonable to assume that a bird in its breeding plumage is at its most attractive to the opposite sex. If so, looking at a Double-crested Cormorant in breeding plumage gives credence to the old saying that there is no accounting for taste.

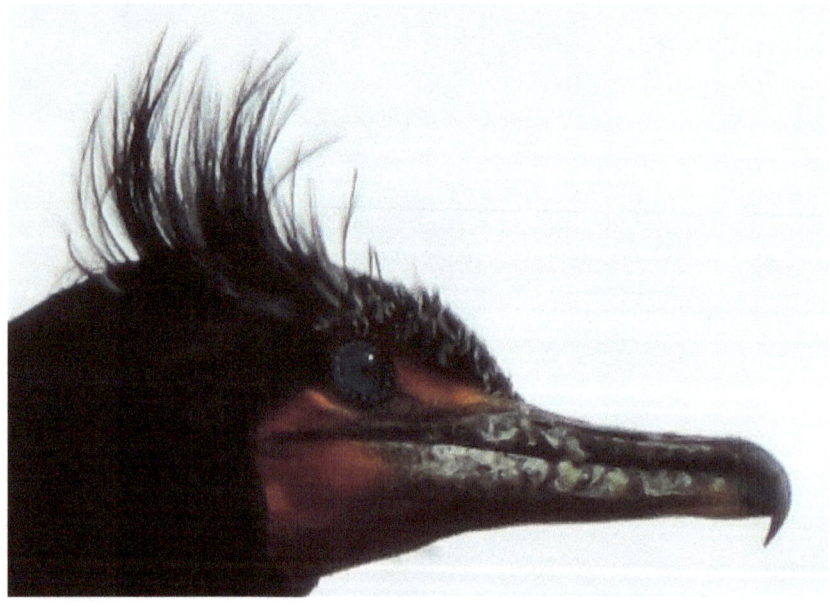

The most charitable thing to say about the breeding plumage is that it reminds one of a bad hair day.

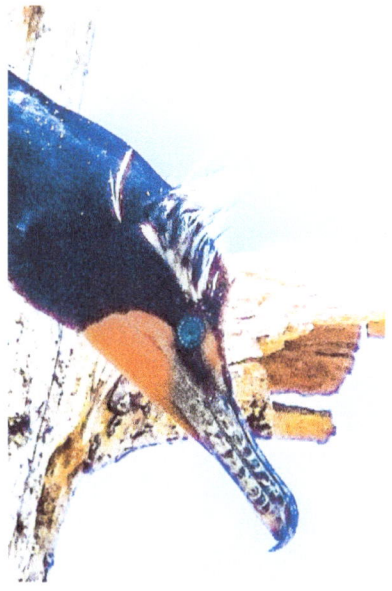

Some references state that the Double-crested Cormorants with white crests live mostly in Alaska. If that is true then some of these birds seen in Arizona make very long migratory flights.

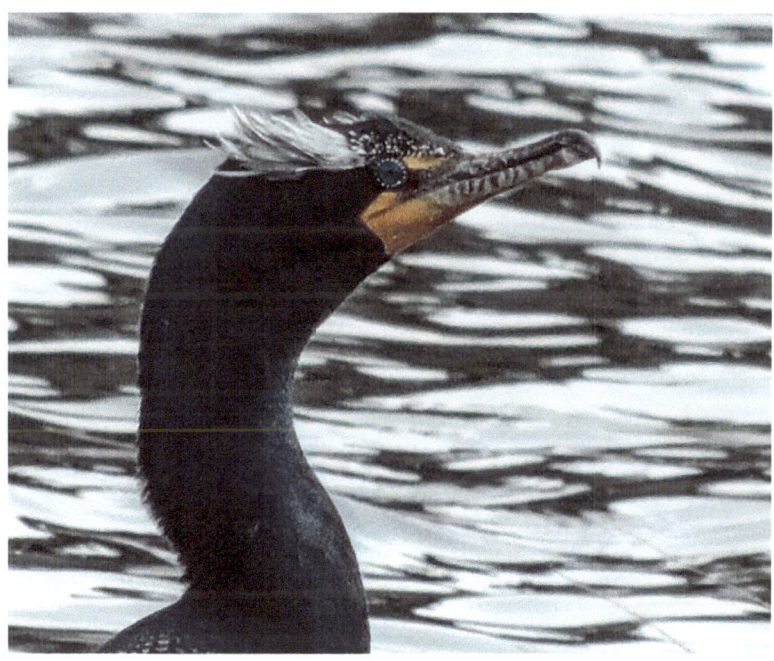

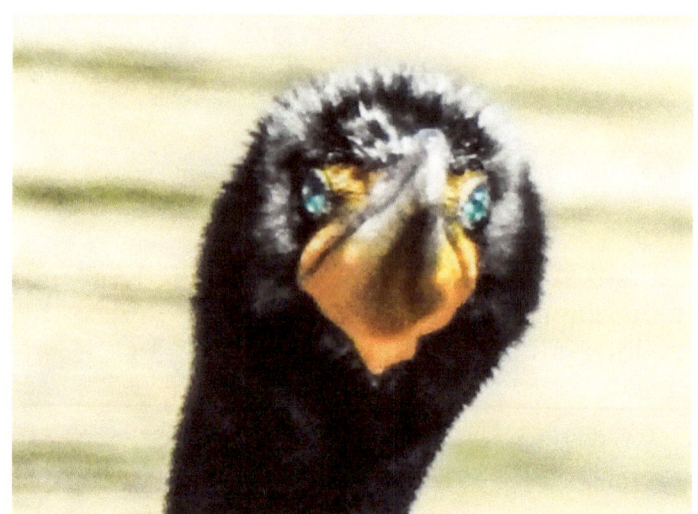

This picture illustrates that these birds have three-dimensional vision – the eyes are widely spaced and face toward the front. Since their primary food is fish this is an absolute necessity because fish can move very fast.